U.S. ARMED FORCES

The U.S. NAVY

TOM STREISSGUTH

LERNER PUBLICATIONS COMPANY / MINNEAPOLIS

CHAPTER OPENER CAPTIONS

Cover: U.S. Navy aircraft fly in a diamond formation above the nuclear-powered aircraft carrier USS *Theodore Roosevelt*.

Ch. 1: A painting of the Continental Navy ship *Columbus* depicts its capture of the British ship *Lord Lifford* off the New England coast.

Ch. 2: All enlistees swear an oath to defend the United States from all enemies. This sailor is reenlisting in front of a memorial to victims of the 1941 Japanese attack on Pearl Harbor, Hawaii.

Ch. 3: Midshipmen perform push-ups as part of their physical training at the U.S. Naval Academy. Physical fitness is important for all members of the navy.

Ch. 4: Navy seamen try to put out a fire set by suspected drug traffickers in the eastern Pacific Ocean. The U.S. Navy routinely patrols the Pacific Ocean in support of the war on drugs.

Lerner Publications Company
A division of Lerner Publishing Group
241 First Avenue North
Minneapolis, MN 55401 U.S.A.

Website address: www.lernerbooks.com

Library of Congress Cataloging-in-Publication Data

Streissguth, Thomas, 1958–
    The U.S. Navy / by Tom Streissguth.
      p.   cm. — (U.S. Armed Forces)
    Includes bibliographical references and index.
    Contents: The history of the Navy—Recruitment—Training—Life in the Navy
    ISBN: 0-8225-1649-7 (lib. bdg. : alk. paper)
    1. United States. Navy—Juvenile literature. [1. United States.
Navy.] I. Title. II. U.S. Armed Forces (Series : Lerner Publications)
  VA58.4.S76 2005
  359'.00973—dc22   2003019641

Manufactured in the United States of America
1 2 3 4 5 6 – JR – 10 09 08 07 06 05

Contents

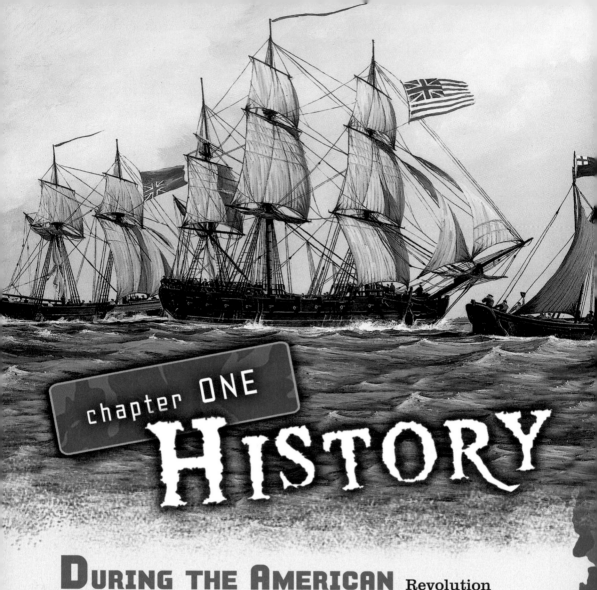

chapter ONE

HISTORY

DURING THE AMERICAN Revolution
(1775–1783), 13 British colonies in North America
fought for their independence from Great Britain.
Great Britain had a powerful land army and the largest
fleet (group) of warships in the world.

On October 13, 1775, the Continental Congress, a
group of colonial leaders, ordered the building of a
Continental Navy to help fight the war. The Congress
appointed Esek Hopkins as the commander and
commissioned (hired) 22 officers as leaders. Hopkins's

ship, *Alfred,* served alongside *Cabot, Andrea Doria, Providence,* and *Columbus.* These and all other warships of the time were sailing ships. They depended on the wind to sail from place to place.

The colonists knew they could never match British firepower at sea. British warships carried rows of powerful cannons on their decks. So the Continental Navy raided other British vessels, such as lightly armed enemy cargo ships. They boarded and captured these prize ships, claimed their cargoes, then sailed the captured ships to their home ports.

RAIDING THE RAIDERS

The United States won its independence in 1783. But the leaders of the young nation knew they needed a permanent, or standing, navy. So in 1794, the U.S. Congress passed a law establishing the U. S. Navy, a permanent national military force.

In 1801 the navy began its first campaign (long

TURTLE

Turtle was the first underwater craft in U.S. military history. American inventor David Bushnell built this submarine in 1776 as a secret weapon for attacking British warships. A sailor inside *Turtle* used a hand-cranked propeller to move the craft forward. He attached an explosive to an enemy ship, then backed away before it exploded.

The first attack of *Turtle* took place in the East River near New York on September 7, 1776. The crewman, Sergeant Ezra Lee of the Continental Army, moved the craft under the stern (rear) of *Eagle*–a British warship. But Lee could not place the explosive on *Eagle*'s copper-covered hull. Lee then unloaded the bomb in the harbor. Its huge explosion alerted the British. *Turtle* had to beat a hasty retreat, chased by several enemy boats. Two similar attempts also failed. *Turtle* was eventually captured and destroyed by the British.

military action). Navy ships sailed to the Mediterranean Sea. They fought against pirates of the Barbary Coast of North Africa. The navy blockaded the port of Tripoli (in modern-day Libya), where many of the pirates had their home port. The campaign lasted until 1805, when the pasha (ruler) of Tripoli surrendered.

THE U.S. MARINE CORPS

The U.S. Congress organized the Marine Corps in 1798. Marines specialize in amphibious invasions— attacking from the sea onto land. Their hard training and skill make them some of the toughest soldiers in the U.S. armed forces. The U.S. government placed the U.S. Marine Corps under the control of the U.S. Navy in 1834. Marines also guard naval bases, surface ships, and submarines. They have their own air force too. During wars large and small, marines are always "the first to fight."

THE WAR OF 1812

After the Barbary Coast campaign, the United States still faced challenges at sea. British ships sometimes impressed U.S. sailors, capturing them and forcing them to serve in the British navy.

Impressment and other issues led to the War of 1812 (1812–1815). The U.S. Navy scored several victories over British warships. On August 19, 1812, USS (U.S. ship) *Constitution* defeated HMS (his majesty's ship) *Guerrière* off the island of Bermuda, in the Atlantic Ocean. The cannonballs of the British guns simply bounced off the thick hull (main body) of *Constitution,* which earned the nickname Old Ironsides.

On June 1, 1813, a fierce battle took place between USS *Chesapeake* and HMS *Shannon. Chesapeake's* commander, James Lawrence, was wounded. He spoke the famous

Chesapeake (right) was swiftly defeated by Shannon (left), despite Captain Lawrence's brave words, "Don't give up the ship!" These words later became the motto for the U.S. Navy.

dying words to his crew: "Don't give up the ship!" But the British captured Chesapeake.

After the War of 1812 ended, the navy began building new kinds of warships. USS Fulton was the first steam-powered warship. Its steam engines allowed it to move about the ocean without having to rely on wind. The navy also replaced cannonballs with explosive shells. Shells could fly farther and easily damage ship hulls. To protect against shells, ship designers began covering their warship hulls with armor plating. These ironclads could ram enemy ships. They could also place explosive charges known as torpedoes right into enemy vessels at the waterline.

THE CIVIL WAR

In the 1800s, the issue of slavery divided the United States. In April 1861, the Civil War (1861–1865) broke out between the Union (the Northern states) and the Confederacy (the Southern states).

The Confederates built an ironclad, CSS *Virginia* (also known as *Merrimac*). The Union navy built a rival, USS *Monitor.* The two ships met in a ferocious battle at Hampton Roads, Virginia, on March 9, 1862. The two ironclads slugged it out, but neither ship could do much damage. After several hours, the two vessels parted ways. The first battle of the ironclads was a stalemate.

The Union Navy helped to capture the Confederate port of New Orleans, Louisiana, in April 1862. The commander, David Farragut, defeated a Confederate battle fleet at the Battle of Mobile Bay in 1864.

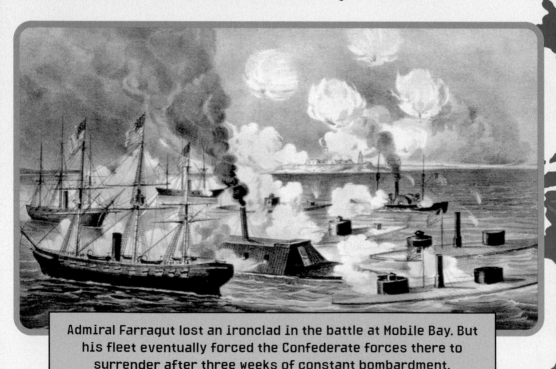

Admiral Farragut lost an ironclad in the battle at Mobile Bay. But his fleet eventually forced the Confederate forces there to surrender after three weeks of constant bombardment.

The U.S. Navy began constructing battleships in 1888. Weighing about 6,000 tons, USS *Texas (above)* was one of the first U.S. battleships built.

Farragut became famous for his stirring command: "Damn the torpedoes! Full speed ahead!"

THE BATTLESHIP ERA

After the Civil War, the U.S. Navy began building battleships. This new kind of warship was made of iron and steel. It carried large revolving gun turrets on its top deck. The United States had expanded across North America to the Pacific Ocean. The new ships patrolled the Atlantic and the Pacific oceans for the United States' new "two-ocean" navy.

DAVY JONES

In sailors' folklore, Davy Jones is the evil spirit believed to rule the souls lost to the bottom of the ocean, which is commonly known as Davy Jones's locker. Because lost items, sunken ships, and sailors who have either drowned or been buried at sea all come to rest there, Davy Jones's locker has come to mean death at sea.

In 1914 a major war broke out in Europe. At first, the United States stayed out of the war, which came to be known as World War I (1914–1918). But German attacks on U.S. ships led the United States to join the war against Germany and its allies in 1917. U.S. battleships fought at sea, while U.S. submarines patrolled beneath the waves. Germany surrendered in 1918.

After the war, the U.S. Navy began to build aircraft carriers—ships that could serve as floating airplane runways. The first U.S. aircraft carrier was USS *Langley.* It had been adapted from a large coal-carrying ship. Aircraft carriers allowed navy ships to attack the enemy—on land or at sea—from longer distances than ever before.

WORLD WAR II AND THE KOREAN WAR

After World War I, battleships remained the U.S. Navy's most important weapon. The navy had also built many smaller warships, such as cruisers and destroyers.

USS *Langley* was launched in 1922. Its flight deck was built on top of the hull of an old supply ship.

On December 7, 1941, a Japanese aircraft carrier fleet attacked U.S. military bases at Pearl Harbor, in the Hawaiian Islands. Japanese bombers sank or damaged every battleship in the Pacific Fleet. After Pearl Harbor, aircraft carriers became the U.S. Navy's most important weapon. The Japanese attack brought the United

USS *Shaw* explodes during the attack on Pearl Harbor in December 1941.

States into World War II (1939–1945). The United States fought the Axis powers of Japan, Germany, and Italy.

World War II was a worldwide war. U.S. forces fought in Europe, Africa, Asia, and the Atlantic and Pacific oceans. In the Atlantic, U.S. Navy ships and submarines fought against German U-boats, deadly submarines that torpedoed and sank hundreds of military and civilian (nonmilitary) ships.

In Europe the armies of Germany had taken over nearly the entire continent by the time the United States joined the fighting. On June 6, 1944, U.S. Navy ships sailing from England took part in D-Day—an amphibious invasion of Normandy, a part of northern France held by the Germans.

The U.S. Navy also took part in amphibious invasions in Italy, southern France, and North Africa. During these landings, battleships sailed offshore, pounding enemy troops and defenses with their powerful guns. While large warships blasted enemy defenses, small landing craft sailed to the beaches. They unloaded troops, tanks, and other equipment. Once troops had fought their way ashore, they began to move inland to push back the German army. Germany surrendered in May 1945.

Meanwhile, in the Pacific, the Japanese had taken control of many Pacific islands and parts of southeastern Asia. In June 1942, U.S. and Japanese carriers fought a massive naval battle for control of Midway Island, northwest of Hawaii. U.S. Navy aircraft, including F4F Wildcat fighters, and SBD Dauntless dive-bombers, sank several Japanese aircraft carriers. U.S. forces won the battle.

SBD Dauntless dive-bombers approach a burning Japanese ship during the battle for Midway Island in 1942.

FIRSTS FOR NAVY WOMEN

In the 1800s, American women were not allowed to be sailors or officers in the U.S. Navy. But opportunities for women in the navy began to take shape in the 1900s.

In 1908 the first women joined the U.S. Navy as part of the Navy Nurse Corps.

During World War I, the first women joined the regular navy, to replace men who were sent to fight in Europe. But women did not serve on combat vessels.

During World War II, many women served their country as WAVES (Women Accepted for Volunteer Emergency Service). They replaced men as air traffic controllers, radio operators, and clerks. Their service helped free navy sailors and fliers for combat duty.

In 1973 the first women pilots graduated from naval flight school.

In 1976 the U.S. Naval Academy welcomed its first female students.

In 1978 USS *Vulcan,* a tender (supply ship), became the first navy nonhospital ship to have women crew members.

In 1979 the 66 women members of *Vulcan's* crew became the first to join an overseas assignment.

In 1988 Deborah S. Gernes became the first woman to command a navy ship.

In 1993 the U.S. Congress passed a law allowing women to serve in combat units.

In 1994 female sailors began to be assigned to fighting ships.

In 2000 Kathleen McGrath became the first woman to skipper (command) a combat ship.

A Japanese diplomat signs a formal surrender aboard USS *Missouri* on September 2, 1945.

The U.S. fleet then began crossing the Pacific Ocean toward Japan. U.S. forces invaded Japanese-held islands and drove out the Japanese defenders there. U.S. forces pushed back the Japanese, taking control of the Philippines and many other islands.

Yet Japanese leaders refused to surrender. So in August 1945, U.S. bombers dropped atomic bombs on two Japanese cities. Soon after, Japan surrendered, ending World War II. The surrender ceremony took place on board USS *Missouri.*

THE COLD WAR AND BEYOND

After World War II, the United States and the Soviet Union (1922–1991) became rivals. Both countries built atomic bombs and prepared to fight a major war against one another. They also created more powerful navies. This period of high tension was known as the Cold War (1945–1991).

In 1950 the army of North Korea invaded its neighbor South Korea. The United States supported South Korea and sent troops to defend its allies. The Soviet Union and China supported North Korea. Early in the Korean War (1950–1953), the U.S. Navy played a key role during an amphibious landing at Inchon. The navy landed marines, who helped to beat back the North Korean invasion. The war ended in stalemate.

After the Korean War, the navy scrapped (took apart) many of its old battleships and built larger aircraft

More than 70,000 troops, 250 ships, and heavy air support took part in the landing at Inchon during the Korean War.

carriers. In the 1960s, the navy launched a fleet of nuclear-powered submarines. These vessels could spend months underneath the surface of the oceans. They could sail anywhere in the world and were difficult for enemy ships to track. They were armed with long-range missiles that carried nuclear weapons— extremely powerful weapons that could wipe out an entire city in seconds. The U.S. Navy's nuclear submarine fleet stood ready to attack the Soviet Union if the Soviets attacked first.

WAR IN VIETNAM AND THE MIDDLE EAST

In the 1960s, the United States tried to help South Vietnam in a civil war with North Vietnam. Communist North Vietnam was trying to

USS *THRESHER* AND THE DSRV

In April 1963, USS *Thresher,* a navy submarine, sank with all 129 hands (personnel) aboard. After the *Thresher* tragedy, the navy designed a vessel specially made to rescue crews from submarines. This vessel is the Deep Submergence Rescue Vehicle (DSRV).

The DSRV can be transported anywhere in the world within 24 hours. It can dive to depths of more than 16,000 feet. Once it reaches the damaged sub, the DSRV attaches itself to a hatch (opening) on the sub's hull. Then the hatch is opened, allowing members of a sub's crew to climb inside the DSRV. The DSRV can carry 24 crew members to the surface at a time.

take over South Vietnam. The United States sent troops, ships, and aircraft to fight alongside the South Vietnamese. U.S. Navy ships sailed along the coast and fired on enemy defenses. Navy pilots flew fighters and bombers on missions over both countries. Navy aircraft included the F-4 Phantom. This powerful fighter could carry many weapons, including bombs and missiles. The F-4 could also reach supersonic speed—faster than the speed of sound.

The U.S. and South Vietnamese forces won every major battle of the Vietnam War. But North Vietnam refused to give up fighting. In 1973 the United States began to remove its forces from Vietnam. In 1975 North Vietnam defeated South Vietnam. Vietnam was united as one country.

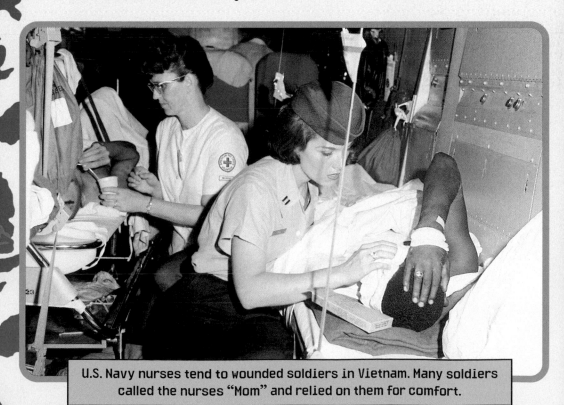

U.S. Navy nurses tend to wounded soldiers in Vietnam. Many soldiers called the nurses "Mom" and relied on them for comfort.

The U.S. Navy saw its next major action in the Middle East. In 1990 the Middle Eastern nation of Iraq invaded its neighbor Kuwait. U.S. president George H. W. Bush called on Iraq's leader, Saddam Hussein, to remove his forces from Kuwait. When Saddam refused, the United States formed a coalition (group) of countries to drive out the Iraqi army. This conflict became known as the Persian Gulf War. U.S. Navy ships moved into the area and prepared to fight. On January 17, 1991, coalition forces attacked. Navy aircraft, such as the F-14 Tomcat fighter, bombed Iraqi targets. Navy warships launched long-range cruise missiles. These powerful missiles can fly hundreds of miles to hit within inches of their targets. A short land campaign then drove Saddam's forces out of Kuwait.

U.S. Navy F-14 Tomcats fly in formation over the Saudi Arabian desert during the 1991 war with Iraq.

The aircraft carrier USS *Nimitz (above)* was among the many U.S. Navy ships stationed in the Persian Gulf in the 1990s.

To keep Saddam from threatening his neighbors again, the United Nations (a worldwide peacekeeping group) ordered the Iraqi leader to disarm parts of his military. U.S. Navy ships patrolled the Persian Gulf near Iraq, making sure no ships brought illegal goods into the country.

Later that year, the Soviet Union collapsed, breaking apart into several independent countries. The Cold War was over. The U.S. government began cutting back its military forces. Many navy ships were removed from service and scrapped.

FIGHTING TERRORISM

On September 11, 2001, terrorists attacked the World Trade Center in New York and the Pentagon, near

Washington, D.C., killing about 3,000 people. The attacks were linked to al-Qaeda, a terrorist group based in Afghanistan. The Taliban, the Afghan government, supported al-Qaeda.

In October 2001, U.S. president George W. Bush ordered the Taliban to hand over all al-Qaeda members living in Afghanistan, including al-Qaeda's leader, Osama bin Laden. When the Taliban refused, U.S. forces invaded the country.

The U.S. Navy played an important role in the war. The closest base for air force planes lay in Kuwait, 1,000 miles to the southwest. And Afghanistan's neighbors would not allow U.S. soldiers to launch a land attack from their countries. For this reason, navy ships did much of the fighting. Navy cruisers and destroyers launched cruise missiles at targets in Afghanistan. Navy aircraft carriers, such as USS *Enterprise,* launched fighter planes and bombers to attack Taliban and

A cruise missile bursts from the sea after being fired from a submarine. Similar missiles were used during the wars against Afghanistan and Iraq.

al-Qaeda bases. Navy SEALs—units of highly trained combat troops— parachuted into Afghanistan to support Afghans fighting against the Taliban. By November 2001, the Taliban government had been destroyed. A new government was set up.

In 2002 U.S. leaders were concerned that Saddam Hussein was still building and holding weapons of mass destruction. The United Nations had ordered Saddam to give up his weapons. But Saddam claimed he had none. Once again, the United States formed a coalition—this time to look for weapons and, eventually, to remove Saddam from power.

In March 2003, President Bush ordered Saddam to leave Iraq. When Saddam refused, coalition forces invaded the country. The war began when navy warships and submarines fired hundreds of cruise missiles on Iraqi targets. Meanwhile, Navy SEAL teams were already inside Iraq. Working in secret, they performed reconnaissance missions, scouting and marking targets for coalition aircraft and missiles to hit.

When coalition forces moved into Iraq, navy aircraft provided close air support (CAS). On CAS missions, F-14 Tomcats, F/A-18 Hornets, and other navy aircraft soared over the battlefield, destroying enemy targets to help coalition troops on the ground.

By April 2003, the Iraqi army had been defeated. U.S. forces captured Saddam in December. Coalition troops remain in Iraq, helping Iraqis to rebuild their country and set up a new government. Navy ships and planes still patrol the Persian Gulf and Iraq, protecting coalition forces.

chapter TWO

RECRUITMENT

THE U.S. NAVY is made up of officers and enlistees. Officers are the navy's leaders. Most officers have college degrees, and they go through training to help them become excellent leaders. Nearly all navy pilots, including fighter pilots, are officers. Enlistees make up most of the navy's personnel.

Like all branches of the U.S. armed forces, the U.S. Navy is a volunteer organization. Enlistment (joining) is open to men and women who are between the ages of 17 and 34. To find out more about navy life, including how to enlist, a person will usually speak with a navy recruiter. The navy has recruiting offices in nearly every city in the United States. Navy recruiters also visit high schools and college campuses to encourage young men and women to learn more about life in the navy.

HEIGHT REQUIREMENTS

The navy will not accept anyone under four feet ten inches tall or anyone taller than six feet six inches. (Shorter people may not be able to operate some navy equipment. Taller people would not be able to live comfortably in a ship's cramped sleeping areas.)

To join the U.S. Navy, enlistees must be a citizen or a permanent resident of the United States. The person cannot be a single parent with custody of a child. All enlistees must also hold a high school diploma (but the navy sometimes makes exceptions). If a person doesn't yet have a high school diploma, the person may be allowed to enlist and then finish high school before going on active duty. All navy enlistees must be in good health and pass a medical examination.

THE NAVY LEAGUE CADET CORPS

There's more than one way to join the navy. Students younger than 17 can still get a taste of navy life and a head start on their navy career. They can join the Navy League Cadet Corps (NLCC) or the Naval Sea Cadet Corps (NSCC).

Boys and girls ages 11 through 13 can join the Navy League Cadet Corps. Cadets (members) meet every week or month at a local training center. A commanding officer instructs them in physical fitness exercises, military life, and seamanship—the skills needed to safely operate a ship. During the summer, cadets travel to a military base for one week of basic training, or boot camp. At boot camp, cadets go through physical training. They practice marching together to develop teamwork and discipline. They also take classes in the history and workings of the U.S. Navy.

If they wish, the cadets of the NLCC can go on to the Naval Sea Cadet Corps when they reach the age of 13. If they have finished one year of the NLCC, they enter the NSCC at a higher rank, or rating.

THE NAVAL SEA CADET CORPS

The Naval Sea Cadet Corps (NSCC) is for cadets ages 13 through 17. Like the NLCC, the NSCC trains

During summer training, a sea cadet learns how to perform a proper lookout watch while aboard an amphibious assault ship.

The secretary of the navy speaks with members of the Naval Sea Cadet Corps.

young people for a future in the navy, the Marine Corps, or the Coast Guard. Cadets drill every week or every month at a local training center—usually a school, community center, or military base. The cadets join a division (surface ship unit), a battalion (construction unit), or a squadron (aviation, or aircraft, unit).

Cadets who train in the NSCC get a head start on a future naval career. They are more likely to win a navy college scholarship. They have a better chance to gain entrance to the U.S. Naval Academy or any other military academy. Also, if they have succeeded in the NSCC, they are better prepared for navy life. As adults they may move up the ratings more quickly than recruits who don't start until after high school.

ACTIVE DUTY VS. THE NAVAL RESERVES

Adult candidates for the navy must choose between joining the full-time navy or the part-time naval reserves. Full-time navy enlistees serve for three years or six years. Navy personnel get 30 days of vacation each year. They can also work toward earning a college degree. The navy offers scholarships to recruits (newcomers) who want to take college courses before joining the service.

The U.S. Naval Reserve is the navy's part-time, back-up naval force. Most members of the reserves have civilian jobs. But they generally serve one weekend per month and spend another two weeks each year in training. Reserve members, called reservists, earn extra money while serving their country. During

Reservists learn how to fire a .50 caliber machine gun in an exercise to prepare them for combat missions.

wartime or in an emergency, reservists may be called to active, full-time duty.

THE U.S. NAVAL ACADEMY

The U.S. Naval Academy at Annapolis, Maryland, trains many of the navy's future officers. The academy is one of the nation's top schools. It accepts only about one out of every ten applicants. To qualify for the academy, candidates must earn good grades in high school and do well on college entrance exams, such as the Scholastic Aptitude Test (SAT). Candidates must also receive a recommendation from their U.S. senator or congressperson.

The tour of duty at the academy lasts four years. During that time, academy students—known as midshipmen, even if they are women—live together in a big dormitory called Bancroft Hall.

Midshipmen follow a very strict daily schedule. They rise at 6:30 A.M. sharp. After breakfast, they attend four morning classes. Midshipmen study English, mathematics, physics, oceanography (the study of the ocean and its resources), geography, and history. In the

THE ASVAB

Those who join the navy must also take the Armed Services Vocational Aptitude Battery (ASVAB) exam. Everyone who enlists in the U.S. military services takes the ASVAB. It consists of 10 short tests that measure knowledge of general science, arithmetic, vocabulary, reading comprehension, simple auto and shop mechanics, and basic electronics. A person's results on the ASVAB help the navy to match each person to the right job. After taking the ASVAB, navy recruits speak with a navy counselor to learn more about their different job options.

afternoon, they march and drill before continuing with their classroom work. The midshipmen then take part in sports or other extracurricular activities. After the evening meal, they study for several hours until "lights out" at 11 P.M. (for first-year students, called plebes) or midnight (for the upper classes).

Midshipmen continue training during the summer. They spend much of their time aboard a navy ship to learn navigation and to take part in military exercises. They spend time on navy submarines and in navy jets.

Graduates become officers in the U.S. Navy or the U.S. Marine Corps. After leaving the academy, they are required to serve on active duty for at least five years. If they choose to leave active duty after this service, they must spend at least three years in the reserves.

Two midshipmen learn about the instruments at a ship's helm (steering wheel) during their summer training.

UNIFORMS

NAVAL PERSONNEL have different uniforms for different occasions, jobs, and roles. In most situations, a sailor or officer's name, rank, and job can all be learned by a quick glance at that person's uniform.

FULL DRESS BLUE

The full dress blue uniform *(left)* is usually worn for ceremonies, such as parades and official navy functions. Officer insignia are sewn on the jacket's lower sleeves. For women, full dress blues include a white shirt and blue skirt.

WHITES

Dress whites *(right)* are worn while performing routine duties in the navy. Whites may also be worn when on shore leave (off-duty time away from the ship). The navy also has a "summer white" uniform with a white shirt and trousers (a white skirt for women). A "tropical white" uniform is for service in tropical climates, where men and women wear white shorts.

KHAKIS

This basic working uniform *(left)* is worn under hazardous conditions or when performing duties in which a normal service dress uniform is impractical.

PRACTICAL BELL-BOTTOMS

The traditional U.S. Navy sailing uniform *(not shown)* includes bell-bottom trousers. The legs of the trousers are flared at the bottom. If a sailor goes overboard, he can slip off the bell-bottom pants easily. He can also tie the legs together. The bell-bottoms allow the trousers to hold more air, which can help the sailor to stay afloat until help comes.

"WORKING GREEN"

"Working green" *(right)* is a uniform of green trousers and jacket and a khaki shirt. It is worn by officers when working in the field or at a military base, under conditions where the uniform might get soiled.

New graduates of the ROTC program stand at attention during their commissioning ceremony.

THE NAVAL RESERVE OFFICERS TRAINING CORPS AND OFFICER CANDIDATE SCHOOL

The Naval Reserve Officers Training Corps, or ROTC, prepares college students for careers as naval officers. Students who join ROTC can win scholarships that pay some or all of their college tuition. The program also offers a regular allowance to students to help pay for day-to-day expenses.

ROTC members spend part of their free time training for service as a navy officer. When they graduate, ROTC candidates become junior officers (ensign or lieutenant). They will spend at least four years on active duty.

Another way to become a navy officer is through the Officer Candidate School in Pensacola, Florida. This course lasts 13 weeks and includes classes as well as military and physical fitness drills. Candidates study naval operations, navy administration, history, weapons systems, and ship management. Those who pass become junior officers in the U.S. Navy.

THE U.S. NAVY ANTHEM
"Anchors Aweigh"

Stand, Navy, out to sea, Fight our battle cry;
We'll never change our course,
     so vicious foe steer shy-y-y-y.
Roll out the TNT, Anchors Aweigh.
     Sail on to victory
And sing their bones to Davy Jones, hooray!

Anchors Aweigh, my boys, Anchors Aweigh.
Farewell to college joys,
     we sail at break of day-ay-ay-ay.
Through our last night on shore,
     drink to the foam.
Until we meet once more. Here's wishing
     you a happy voyage home.

chapter THREE

TRAINING

FOR ALL RECRUITS, navy life begins with
recruit training, or boot camp. Training takes place at
the Naval Recruit Training Center, in Great Lakes,
Illinois. There, enlistees prepare for the physical and
mental demands of military service.

Recruit training begins with three to ten days of
processing, also known as p-days. During p-days, recruits
learn the basic routine. They receive physical and dental
exams and get haircuts. Men have their hair shaved off,
while women have their hair cut short. Recruits also

receive their navy gear, including clothing, shoes, towels, notebooks, writing materials, and other items. Once p-days are over, the eight weeks of actual training begin.

Recruit training teaches the value of teamwork. Recruits learn to live and work as a team. In combat situations, their lives may depend on teamwork. Recruits live together in dormitories, start the day together, work out together, attend classes together, and eat their meals together. They cooperate in carrying out their tasks and learn how to depend on each other.

The recruits are organized into divisions. Competing together, the members of these divisions work to earn awards for their athletic ability,

Recruits sing as they run during a battle stations drill. The drill involves running from station to station to complete various tasks as a team. All recruits must complete battle stations before graduating from boot camp.

classroom ability, drill precision, and overall excellence. The competition drives each division to work together to succeed.

At boot camp, navy recruits also concentrate on physical fitness. Recruits run and do calisthenics (exercises to develop strength and endurance). They also learn basic self-defense—how to fight the enemy in hand-to-hand combat. Trainers yell instruction and encouragement and punish laziness with stern lectures and more hard exercise. The recruits also take part in military drills—marching, turning, and standing in rank and file. By the end of the day, recruits need a good night's sleep.

A sailor practices the self-defense moves he has learned.

Classroom instruction teaches the basics of navy service—how the navy is organized, how it operates, its weapons, rates, and routines. Recruits learn how to take orders, how to salute, how to stand sentry (guard), how to respond in an emergency, and much more.

AFTER BASIC TRAINING

By the end of basic training, recruits are in excellent physical condition. They are used to rising early and spending hours performing exercise and physical activity. They have learned how to give a salute and how to obey orders from a superior officer.

Making it through boot camp is only the beginning. Next, recruits must train for their future jobs in the navy. Some recruits enter the apprenticeship program, where they will train for basic and important tasks. These tasks include learning how to maintain equipment, how to handle navigation and weapons systems, or how to perform office duties. Other recruits move on to specialized schools, where the navy trains them for more advanced and complicated tasks.

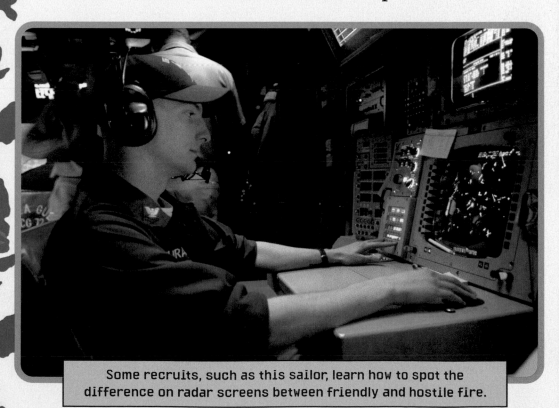

Some recruits, such as this sailor, learn how to spot the difference on radar screens between friendly and hostile fire.

Seamen practice patching broken pipes during a safety-training event aboard their ship.

For enlistees, the three basic and important careers are seaman, fireman, and airman. Both men and women hold these jobs, and women sailors are called seamen, firemen, or airmen.

Navy recruits start out with the rank of seaman. The able seaman, in history and in modern times, helps to sail a seagoing ship. He or she must know how to handle a variety of onboard equipment. Seamen train to use shipboard weapons systems, navigational equipment, and radar.

The job of airman was created in the 1900s, when the navy began flying military aircraft. The modern airman maintains and repairs the navy's jets and helicopters. Airmen receive specialized training in subjects like aircraft maintenance, aircraft weapons systems, electronics, and computer software.

Firemen are the navy's mechanics. They operate the engines and machinery aboard ship, including diesel and gas engines, turbines, and boilers. Depending on their job, firemen train to operate and repair different kinds of equipment.

NAVY SCHOOLS

The navy's specialized schools include the Nuclear Power School in Charleston, South Carolina. At this school, personnel learn the basics of nuclear power. After this course, candidates attend a Nuclear Power Training Unit (NPTU) in Charleston or in northern New York. At the NPTU, students get hands-on experience in how to handle nuclear reactors—the engines that power nuclear submarines and aircraft carriers.

Students aboard a nuclear-powered aircraft carrier take an exam.

TOOLS OF THE TRADE

THE U.S. NAVY HAS THE LARGEST and most powerful fleet in the world. Navy ships, boats, and aircraft come in a variety of shapes and sizes. They perform a variety of roles and missions.

SURFACE SHIPS

USS *Bunker Hill (above)* is equipped with the Aegis radar system, which uses sound waves to track more than 100 targets at the same time. Aegis means "protection," and the Aegis system is designed to protect surface ships against enemy missiles and attacks. Aegis warships have antiaircraft and antimissile missiles, which can shoot down enemy planes and missiles.

AIRCRAFT CARRIERS

Aircraft carriers *(left)* are the backbone of the U.S. Navy fleet. The navy's eight Nimitz-class aircraft carriers are the largest in the world. These ships are 1,092 feet long with flight decks spanning 252 feet. Two nuclear reactors power the carriers. Each Nimitz-class vessel can carry 85 aircraft and holds a crew of 3,200, with an aircrew of 2,480.

SUBMARINES

The Seawolf-class attack submarine can fight enemy surface ships and submarines. It carries Tomahawk cruise missiles as well as torpedoes, mines, and unmanned underwater vehicles. These subs also gather intelligence (information) on enemy movements and help deliver special forces teams—like Navy SEAL teams—to land missions.

AIRCRAFT

The navy operates a large fleet of fighter planes, as well as reconnaissance aircraft. The newest and most powerful of these is the F/A-18 E/F Super Hornet *(above)*. The letter "F" in the Hornet's designation stands for "fighter," meaning the Hornet was designed to battle other aircraft. "A" stands for "attack," meaning the Hornet also has the ability to strike targets on the ground. The Super Hornet can fly up to an altitude of 50,000 feet and reach speeds of Mach 1.8 (1.8 times the speed of sound).

MISSILES

Tomahawk cruise missiles *(above)* allow navy surface ships to strike enemy targets far inland. Missiles carry their own navigational equipment and usually fly very low, which makes them hard to shoot down. Some navy submarines are equipped with Trident long-range missiles that can carry nuclear warheads (explosives) up to 4,500 miles at speeds reaching 13,500 miles per hour.

The Submarine Officer Basic Course in Groton, Connecticut, trains future submarine officers. Students learn how to serve on these underwater vessels. Submarines have their own particular power systems, navigation systems, radar systems, and weapons that are very different from those of surface ships.

Most U.S. Navy pilots are officers. Fliers take flight training at the Naval Aviation Schools Command in Pensacola. They begin by learning the basics of flying during a six-week air indoctrination (instruction) course. Pilots then move on to practice their skills in basic flight training. Instruction combines classroom

A pilot sits in an F/A-18 Hornet flight simulator, a device that teaches pilots how to fly by imitating real flying circumstances.

work, work with computerized flight simulators, and flying actual aircraft. By the time a candidate reaches advanced training, the person has become skilled in flying a certain type of aircraft, such as the F-14 Tomcat or the F/A-18 Hornet. Pilots-in-training also learn how to complete many types of missions, including bombing missions, search-and-rescue missions, or reconnaissance missions.

Officers in the Navy Civil Engineer Corps learn to build and design onshore facilities, such as buildings, harbors, bridges, and maintenance and repair facilities. The Civil Engineering Program is open to college students who have finished at least two years of higher education. When they complete their college studies, they begin Officer Candidate School and then train at the navy's Civil Engineering Corps Officers School in Port Hueneme, California.

When sailors complete their training course, they are assigned to a unit. They may be deployed (assigned) overseas, or they may serve in the United States.

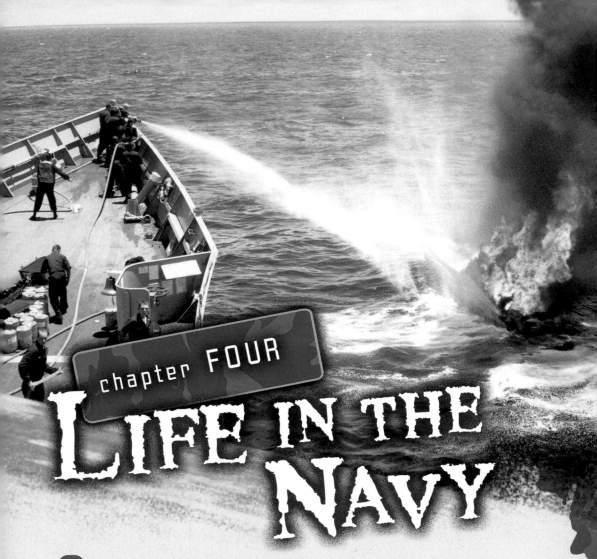

chapter FOUR

LIFE IN THE NAVY

AFTER FINISHING their basic training,
navy recruits are assigned to a command (ship or shore
base). Commands are divided into fleet operation
commands and shore commands. Navy shore
commands include naval air stations, navy ports and
shipyards, naval training centers, navy hospitals, and
the U.S. Naval Academy. Those who sail—or serve
aboard the U.S. Navy fleet—join fleet operation
commands. They work on a schedule known as a
rotation. They spend a certain amount of time onshore,

then rotate to a command at sea. The usual length of deployment at sea is six months. In time of war or crisis, a ship and its crew may spend more than six months at sea.

Navy duty can take officers and enlisted men to one of the five U.S. Navy battle fleets and their areas of operation. These include the Second Fleet at Norfolk, Virginia, which operates in the Atlantic Ocean. The Third Fleet operates out of San Diego, California, and patrols the central and eastern Pacific Ocean. The Fifth Fleet, based in Manama, Bahrain, sails the Persian Gulf. The Sixth Fleet in Naples, Italy, patrols the

A sailor aboard USS *Coronado*, the Third Fleet command ship, keeps watch near the entrance of San Diego Harbor in southern California.

Mediterranean Sea. The Seventh Fleet in Yokosuka, Japan, sails the western Pacific Ocean and the Indian Ocean.

The navy keeps very strict hours. At the same time each morning, sailors report to their commanding officer. Then they take their stations. A station might be a gun turret, a commander's post, or a computer console.

NAVY TIME: OFFICIAL TIME
The U.S. Navy doesn't just defend the nation at sea. It also has the job of keeping time for the nation. A master clock at the Naval Observatory in Washington, D.C., keeps official time for the United States. The observatory also tracks the movements of the sun, moon, planets, and stars.

The navy has an entire book of regulations, known as *The Bluejacket's Manual.* This book covers nearly every possible part of navy life. According to navy tradition, there are two ways of doing things—the navy way and the wrong way. Members of the navy are expected to carry out their tasks "by the book."

NAVY JOBS

About 95 percent of U.S. Navy personnel are enlistees. Most of these people perform the important day-to-day tasks of seamen, firemen, and airmen. Enlistees keep the U.S. Navy running smoothly.

The U.S. Navy also has many specialized jobs. Electronics technicians operate the equipment that controls navigation, weapons, and radar systems aboard ship. Weapons technicians handle naval guns, torpedoes, or missiles. They also handle the bombs and weaponry carried by navy planes.

Nuclear propulsion technicians handle the nuclear reactors that power many navy ships and submarines. Radar and sonar operators control the equipment that uses radio waves to scan the skies and the seas for enemy ships, planes, missiles, and submarines.

Medics care for the sick and wounded in navy hospitals and on board ships. Disbursing clerks keep records of pay and other benefits. Air traffic controllers track jets and helicopters that are taking off and landing at navy ports and aboard aircraft carriers. The navy also has computer programmers, oceanographers (people who study the ocean), photographers, journalists, instructors, chaplains (clergymen), and many other important jobs. All personnel wear insignia that identify their specialty.

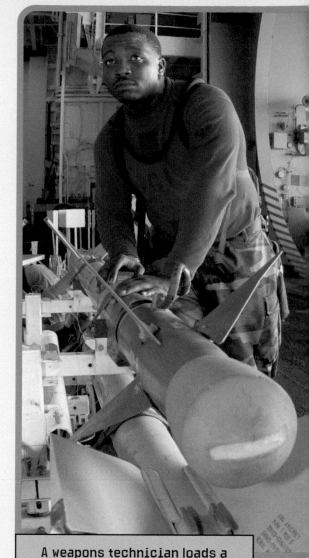

A weapons technician loads a Sidewinder missile onto a ship's weapons elevator.

INSIGNIA

LIKE ALL OF THE U.S. ARMED FORCES, the U.S. Navy is organized according to rank. A person of lower rank is required to follow the orders of a person of higher rank. For example, a seaman recruit, the lowest rank in the navy, must follow the orders of a petty officer or an ensign. The highest naval rank is (four-star) admiral. Here are a number of insignia, starting with the lowest rank and moving up to the highest.

ENLISTED PERSONNEL

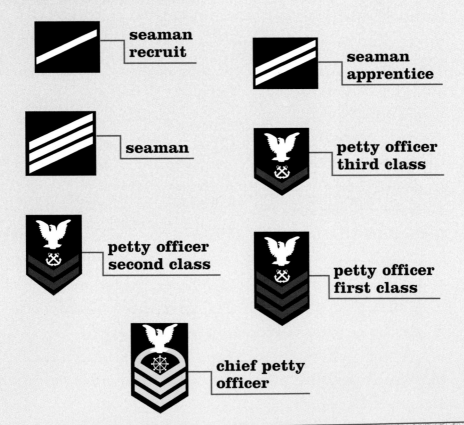

seaman recruit

seaman apprentice

seaman

petty officer third class

petty officer second class

petty officer first class

chief petty officer

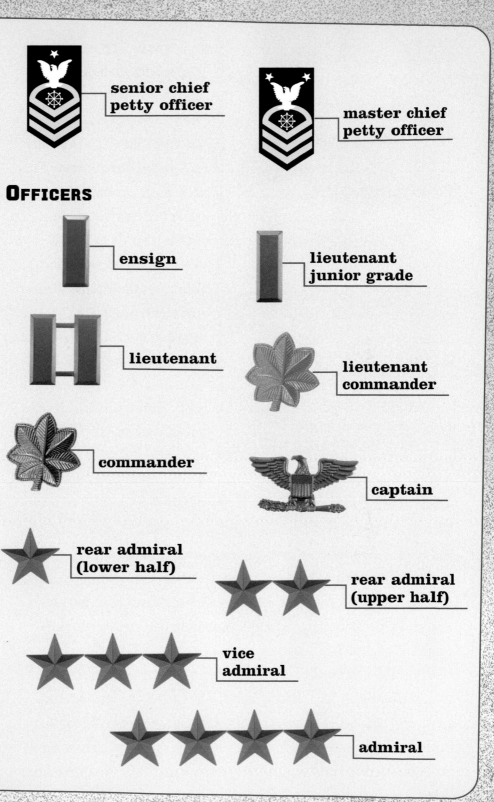

senior chief
petty officer

master chief
petty officer

OFFICERS

ensign

lieutenant
junior grade

lieutenant

lieutenant
commander

commander

captain

rear admiral
(lower half)

rear admiral
(upper half)

vice
admiral

admiral

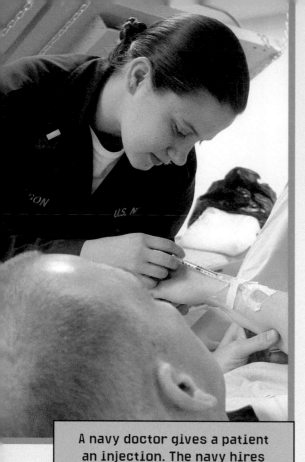

A navy doctor gives a patient an injection. The navy hires many doctors and nurses.

Naval officers are divided into three groups, based on their jobs. Unrestricted line officers are commanders. They command ships at sea, specialized warfare units (such as SEAL units), or engineering teams. Restricted line officers perform specialized tasks but are not given overall commands. Members of the staff corps include doctors, dentists, lawyers, and chaplains.

THE FUTURE OF THE U.S. NAVY

The U.S. Navy is the most powerful single military force in history. The navy operates dozens of submarines, hundreds of large ships, and thousands of aircraft. When trouble breaks out around the world, the president of the United States often calls on the nearest naval fleet to take action.

The U.S. Navy's role became more important after the September 11, 2001, terrorist attacks. Instead of training to fight a huge war, the navy is training for smaller battles against small groups of terrorists and the countries that support them. The U.S. Navy is also building equipment to help with this new job. This equipment includes new submarines, warships, aircraft, and weapon systems.

FUTURE NAVY VESSELS

The Virginia-class new attack submarine (NAS) is the U.S. Navy's newest type of submarine. The NAS is designed to perform many different kinds of missions. It can sail in the deep, open ocean or operate in shallow waters close to shore. The NAS can perform antiship and antisubmarine tasks, meaning it can attack and destroy enemy ships and submarines. It can also carry cruise missiles for striking enemy land targets. It also has special equipment for spying on enemy targets. The NAS is also designed to help U.S. Navy SEALs

This drawing shows the new Virginia-class attack submarine being built for the U.S. Navy.

reach their targets. Each Virginia-class sub is equipped with a small, detachable submarine that SEALs can use to sneak ashore.

The navy is also building unmanned underwater vehicles (UUVs). UUVs are remote-controlled underwater vessels. An operator on a ship or onshore controls the UUV with a computer. The U.S. Navy uses these vehicles for dangerous jobs such as finding enemy mines—small explosive devices placed in the water to destroy ships.

The navy is also developing new ships for amphibious landings. The new San Antonio-class amphibious assault ship will soon enter service. These new ships have landing pads for helicopters, a dock for landing craft to load and unload marines, and missile launchers for attacking land targets.

Navy officials are working on a new kind of destroyer—the Zumwalt-class land attack destroyer. This fast and powerful vessel will battle enemy ships and submarines. But its key role will be providing support for ground troops. The Zumwalt can sail in shallow waters near coastlines. It carries cruise missiles and other land-attack missiles to help clear the way for ground forces. The Zumwalt is also being designed with stealth technology. It will have an unusual shape that will make it difficult to detect with radar equipment.

While its ships and equipment will change over the years, the navy will always need good sailors and officers. Each year thousands of young women and men volunteer to be a part of the world's most powerful fighting force. They will join the nearly 380,000 people who proudly serve their country in the U.S. Navy.

THE BLUE ANGELS

The Blue Angels are the U.S. Navy's flight demonstration squadron. The team performs its spectacular high-speed maneuvers at air shows around the world. Navy leaders created the Blue Angels at the end of World War II to demonstrate the skills of navy pilots and the abilities of the navy's top fighter aircraft. The team's first performance took place over Jacksonville, Florida, in June 1946. Since then, the Blue Angels have performed for more than 380 million people.

The Blue Angels demonstration team flies six F/A-18 Hornets. A top navy pilot flies each aircraft. The team practices during the winter months, before performing in shows across North America for the rest of the year.

Blue Angel performances last about 75 minutes. During the show, the team executes a variety of exciting high-speed maneuvers, reaching altitudes as high as 15,000 feet and as low as 50 feet. These include flying in extremely close formation—just a few feet apart—and performing many difficult twists, turns, and rolls (above).

STRUCTURE

THE PRESIDENT OF THE UNITED STATES is the commander in chief of all of the U.S. armed forces. The secretary of defense is directly responsible for the armed forces and reports directly to the president. The person in charge of the navy is a civilian, the secretary of the navy. The navy's highest-ranking military post is chief of naval operations (CNO). The CNO is a four-star admiral and a member of the Joint Chiefs of Staff, a group of the top military commanders who advise the president on military matters.

PRESIDENT OF THE UNITED STATES
SECRETARY OF DEFENSE
SECRETARY OF THE NAVY
CHIEF OF NAVAL OPERATIONS

FLEET OPERATION COMMANDS	SHORE COMMANDS

The U.S. Navy is divided into large groups called commands. A four-star admiral is in charge of each command. Commands are either fleet operation commands (groups of ships) or shore commands (bases and support units). Fleet operations are organized into four commands, each of which controls one or two fleets. A three-star vice admiral commands each fleet, and the fleets may move from one operational area to another as required.

TIMELINE

1775   The Continental Congress calls for the creation of the Continental Navy to fight for independence from the British.

1778   During the Revolutionary War (1775–1783), John Paul Jones sails a squadron of colonial ships to the British Isles to raid British ports and homes.

1794   An act of Congress establishes the U.S. Navy. The act authorizes the building of six frigates (large warships).

1798   The Department of the Navy is formed, and the U.S. Marine Corps is established.

1801–1805   Navy squadrons sail to the Mediterranean Sea to destroy the pirates of the Barbary Coast (North Africa).

1812   After U.S. sailors are forced to serve aboard British naval ships, the United States and Britain fight the War of 1812 (1812–1815).

1862   On March 9, the first battle between ironclad warships takes place in Hampton Roads, Virginia, between the Union ship *Monitor* and the Confederate ship *Virginia*. On April 25, a Union Navy squadron under Admiral David Farragut accepts the surrender of New Orleans, Louisiana, an important Confederate city.

1908   Women first join the navy as part of the Navy Nurse Corps.

1917–1918   During World War I (1914–1918), the United States operates airships, or aircraft filled with light helium gas. These craft fly over enemy lines for reconnaissance and bombing missions.

1941   On December 7, the Japanese launch a surprise attack on U.S. military bases at Pearl Harbor, Hawaii. All eight of the Pacific fleet's heavy battleships are sunk or heavily damaged. The next day, the United States declares war on Japan and enters World War II (1939–1945).

1942   The navy defeats the Japanese carrier force at the Battle of Midway.

1945	U.S. Navy fleet admiral Chester Nimitz is one of the people accepting the Japanese surrender aboard the battleship USS *Missouri*.
1950	The navy leads the amphibious landings at Inchon, Korea, during the Korean War (1950–1953).
1954	The nuclear-powered submarine USS *Nautilus* enters service.
1960s–1974	During the Vietnam War, navy battleships strike enemy positions on land. Navy planes based on aircraft carriers carry out missions over South Vietnam and North Vietnam.
1991	During the Persian Gulf War, U.S. Navy carriers carry out hundreds of bombing and reconnaissance missions from the Persian Gulf and Indian Ocean.
2001	After the September 11 terrorist attacks on the United States, navy aircraft attack al-Qaeda terrorist camps and Taliban forces in Afghanistan. Navy SEAL teams also hunt down terrorists in Afghanistan.
2003	Cruise missiles fired from navy submarines and warships begin the war against Iraq. Navy SEAL teams land in Iraq to organize coalition forces fighting against Iraqi forces.
2004	Coalition forces remain in Iraq to help rebuild the country.

GLOSSARY

admiral: the highest navy rank

deployment: moving a navy ship or command to a new position for a tour of duty

drilling: parade (marching) and physical exercise that helps to develop and maintain discipline

enlisted personnel: armed forces members who are not officers. Most navy members are enlisted personnel. The lowest enlisted rank is seaman recruit, or Rate E-1. The highest enlisted rate is E-9, master chief petty officer of the navy.

enlistment: joining the armed forces

fleet: the largest group of navy ships and aircraft serving under a single commander

impressment: to be captured and forced to serve aboard a ship at sea

leave: an authorized vacation from military service

midshipmen: students of the U.S. Naval Academy

officer: a man or woman responsible for command of personnel, equipment, and/or weapons. Officer ranks progress from the lowest (ensign) to fleet admiral, the highest rank.

plebes: first-year students of the U.S. Naval Academy

rating: a person's rank or job title in the navy

sailor: a man or woman who takes part in seagoing activities

scrap: to take out of service and take apart a piece of equipment, such as a ship

standing: describes a permanent navy, in service whether the country is at war or not

tender: a ship responsible for supply of another ship or fleet

FAMOUS PEOPLE

Jimmy Carter (born 1924) Jimmy Carter, the 39th president of the United States (1977–1981), is a native of Georgia. He graduated from the U.S. Naval Academy in 1946 and served for two years as an officer aboard battleships. He then was transferred to submarine duty aboard USS *Pomfret* in the Pacific Ocean. Carter served on board the nuclear submarine USS *Sea Wolf*. He retired from the navy in 1953.

Commodore Stephen Decatur (1779–1820) Born in Philadelphia, Pennsylvania, Decatur was one of the U.S. Navy's first heroes. He commanded a fleet in the Mediterranean Sea during the campaign against the Barbary States from 1801 to 1805. Decatur also took part in the victory of USS *United States* against the British ship *Macedonia* during the War of 1812. He was the youngest man ever to hold the rank of captain, at the age of 25. He was killed by his rival, James Barron, in a duel in 1820.

Admiral David Farragut (1801–1870) At the age of 12, Farragut sailed as a prize master—a sailor who skippered captured ships into port. Although he was from the Confederate state of Tennessee, he served in the Union Navy during the Civil War, commanding a naval blockade of Confederate ports in the Gulf of Mexico. He led the capture of the Confederate city of New Orleans in the spring of 1862, commanded Union ships on the Mississippi River, and triumphed at the Battle of Mobile Bay in 1864.

Admiral William F. "Bull" Halsey (1882–1959) Born in Elizabeth, New Jersey, William F. Halsey earned the nickname "Bull" for his aggressive style of fighting. During World War I, Halsey commanded destroyers in the North Atlantic Ocean. During the World War II campaign against Japan in the Pacific, Halsey commanded naval forces in the Solomon Islands, the Philippines, and the island of Okinawa.

John Paul Jones (1747–1792) Born in Kirkcudbrightshire, Scotland, Jones is often called the "Father of the American Navy." He led a squadron of Continental Navy ships during the American Revolution. Commanding *Bonhomme Richard,* Jones captured the British ship HMS *Serapis* on September 23, 1779, after a long and vicious battle.

John F. Kennedy (1917–1963) The 35th president of the United States (1961–1963), Kennedy was born in Brookline, Massachusetts. He joined the navy in September 1941, shortly before the attack on Pearl Harbor. During World War II, he became famous for his heroic actions as commander of a PT (patrol torpedo) boat in the Pacific Ocean. After leaving the navy in 1945, he was elected to the U.S. House of Representatives as a Democratic congressman from Massachusetts. He was elected to the presidency in 1960. Kennedy was assassinated in November 1963.

Fleet Admiral Ernest J. King (1878–1956) Born in Lorain, Ohio, King took part in the early building of naval airpower. In 1930 he commanded the aircraft carrier USS *Lexington*. King later served as chief of the Bureau of Aeronautics in 1933 and went on to become commander of the navy's Pacific carrier fleet in 1938. After the Japanese attack on Pearl Harbor, President Roosevelt appointed King commander in chief of the U.S. fleet. He directed all naval operations during the war.

Captain Kathleen McGrath (1952–2002) Born in Columbus, Ohio, Captain McGrath was the first woman to command a U.S. Navy warship. In the late 1990s and early 2000s, she commanded the guided missile frigate USS *Jarrett.* Her ship searched the Persian Gulf for ships breaking a ban on oil shipments from Iraq.

Fleet Admiral Chester Nimitz (1885–1966) Born in Fredericksburg, Texas, Nimitz served as the commander in chief of the U.S. Pacific fleet during World War II. He led the fleet to important victories against Japan at the Battles of Coral Sea, Midway, and in the Solomon Islands. In 1944 he was promoted to fleet admiral—a new rank and the highest navy rank.

David Robinson (born 1965) Born in Key West, Florida, Robinson was an All-Star center for the San Antonio Spurs of the National Basketball Association (NBA) from 1989 to 2003. He is a graduate of the U.S. Naval Academy. He was a nine-time NBA All-Star and led the Spurs to two NBA championships in 1999 and 2003. Robinson also played on three U.S. Olympic basketball squads and holds the all-time U.S. Olympic records in points, rebounds, and blocks.

BIBLIOGRAPHY

Holland, W. J. *The Navy.* Westport, CT: Hugh Lauter Levin Associates, 2000.

Humble, Richard. *U. S. Navy.* New York: Arco Publishing, Inc., 1985.

Mack, William P. *Naval Ceremonies, Customs and Traditions.* Annapolis, MD: U.S. Naval Institute, 1981.

FURTHER READING

Dartford, Mark. *Fighter Planes.* Minneapolis: Lerner Publications Company, 2003.

___. *Helicopters.* Minneapolis: Lerner Publications Company, 2003.

___. *Missiles and Rockets.* Minneapolis: Lerner Publications Company, 2003.

___. *Warships.* Minneapolis: Lerner Publications Company, 2003.

Doyle, Kevin. *Aircraft Carriers.* Minneapolis: Lerner Publications Company, 2003.

___. *Submarines.* Minneapolis: Lerner Publications Company, 2003.

Fine, Jill. *Life inside the Naval Academy.* New York: Children's Press, 2002.

Gaines, Ann Graham. *The Navy in Action.* Berkeley Heights, NJ: Enslow Publishers, Inc., 2001.

Holden, Henry M. *Navy Combat Aircraft and Pilots.* Berkeley Heights, NJ: Enslow Publishers, Inc., 2002.

Hole, Dorothy. *The Navy and You.* New York: Crestwood House, 1993.

Van Orden, M. D. *U.S. Navy Ships and Coast Guard Cutters.* Annapolis, MD: Naval Institute Press, 2000.

WEBSITES

Navy.com: Explore the Navy: Aircraft Carriers
<http://www.navy.com/aircraftcarriers>
This site features information and photos about aircraft carriers, the backbone of the U.S. Navy fleet. Learn more about the navy's different classes, or types, of carriers, the many different kinds of aircraft they support, and the crews who keep these giant ships running smoothly.

Navy.com: Explore the Navy: Cruisers and Destroyers
<http://www.navy.com/cruisers>
Visit this site to learn more about the navy's fleet of surface warships, including cruisers, destroyers, and frigates. Read about the Ticonderoga-class cruiser, the most advanced warship in the world, as well as the weapons systems used in all these fighting vessels.

The Official Blue Angels Website
<http://www.blueangels.navy.mil/>
Learn more about the Blue Angels, the U.S. Navy's air demonstration squadron. This site features photos, an up-to-date performance schedule, and information on the history of the Blue Angels, its pilots and support teams, and the F/A-18 Hornet.

The U.S. Naval Academy
<http://www.usna.edu>
Visit the main website of the U.S. Naval Academy, with information on academics, admissions, daily schedules, plebe (first-year) summer, and extracurricular and sports activities.

The U.S. Naval Sea Cadets Corps and Navy League Cadet Corps
<http://www.seacadets.org>
This website has information on the Sea Cadets, a branch of the navy for recruits ages 11 to 17 years, and about the Navy League Cadet Corps for students ages 11 through 13. The site has pages on Sea Cadet activities and a map of Sea Cadet camps throughout the United States, Guam, and Puerto Rico.

The U.S. Navy
<http://www.navy.mil>
The navy's website has information on current navy operations as well as detailed descriptions of how the navy is organized and operated around the world. The site also covers navy recruitment and military and civilian navy careers.

INDEX

ABOUT THE AUTHOR

Tom Streissguth has written more than 50 books of nonfiction—biography, history, geography, and books on current events—for young readers. He studied music at Yale University and has worked as an editor, teacher, and journalist. He was born in Washington, D.C., grew up in Minneapolis, Minnesota, and currently lives in Florida.

PHOTO ACKNOWLEDGMENTS

The images in this book are used with the permission of: © U.S. Naval Photos provided by Navy Visual News Service, Washington, D.C., pp. 4, 9, 10, 12, 23, 25, 26, 27, 29, 30 (both), 31 (left), 35, 36, 37, 38, 39, 40 (left), (both), 42, 44, 45, 47, 50, 51, 53; © Peter Newark's American Pictures, p. 7; Library of Congress, pp. 8 (LC-USZC2-2524), 14 (LC-USZ62-2035-3); Defense Visual Information Center, pp. 11, 16, 19, 31 (right), 40 (right); National Archives, p. 15; © Bettmann/CORBIS, p. 17; © CORBIS, pp. 18, 20; © Anna Clopet/CORBIS, p. 34; © Erin Liddell/Independent Picture Service, pp. 48 (all), 49 (top); © Todd Strand/ Independent Picture Service, p. 49 (officers insignia).

Cover: © U.S. Naval Photos provided by Navy Visual News Service, Washington, D.C.